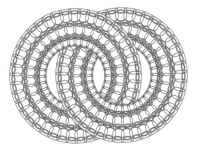

AGAINST
WHICH

ROSS GAY

AGAINST
WHICH

ROSS GAY

CavanKerry ❖ Press LTD.

Library of Congress Cataloging-in-Publication Data

Gay, Ross, 1974-
Against which / Ross Gay. – 1st ed.
p. cm.
ISBN-13: 978-1-933880-00-6
ISBN-10: 1-933880-00-7
I. Title.

PS3607.A9857A73 2006
813'.6–dc22

2006018743

Cover and text design by Peter Cusack

Cover art: "But to the Boy" © 2004 Ross Gay and Kim Thomas

First Edition 2006

Printed in Canada

CavanKerry Press Ltd.
Fort Lee, New Jersey
www.cavankerrypress.org

ACKNOWLEDGEMENTS

American Poetry Review: "Song of the Pig Who Gave the Poet, Age 3,
        Worms," "Let Me Be," and "Two Bikers Embrace on Broad Street"

American Poetry Review: Philadelphia Edition: "The Voice"

Atlanta Review: "Dead Hair" and "The Rearing Back"

Cave Canem VIII: "The Heaven"

Gathering Ground: Cave Canem 10th Anniversary Anthology: "Unclean.
        Make Me." forthcoming

Columbia: A Journal of Poetry and Art: "The Hernia"

The Drunken Boat (online): "Ruptured Aneurysm" and "The First Breath"

www.exittheapple.com: "For a Young Emergency Room Doctor"

Fulcrum: "Man Tries to Commit Suicide With a Crossbow" and "Dying is an Art"

Global City Review: "Broken Mania"

Harvard Review: "Marionette"

Margie: The American Journal of Poetry: "Beat Him Again," "One Eye Gone
        Black," "Summer," "Late October in Easton," "At Burger King,"
        "Thank You," and "Postcard: Lynching of an Unidentified Man, circa
        1920"

Natural Bridge: "Until Now," "The Poet Dreams of His Father" and "Litany"

North American Review: "Alzheimer's"

Sow's Ear Poetry Review: "It Starts at Birth"

Sulfur: "Bar-b-q" (previously titled "On 60 Minutes")

"Cousin Drowses on the Flight to Kuwait," "Dying is an Art," "How to Fall in
Love with Your Father," "Man Tries to Commit Suicide with a Crossbow" and
"Unclean. Make Me." all appear on *From the Fishouse: An Audio Archive of
Emerging Poets,* edited by Matt O'Donnell.

I would like to thank my teachers: Thomas Lux, Joan Larkin, Marie Howe,
David Rivard, Lee Upton, and especially Gerald Stern. Secondly, there have
been numerous friends who have been indispensable in the creation of this
book: Pat, Ruthie, Aracelis, Curtis, Wally, Simone, Ed, Elaine, Anne Marie,
Sarah, Jay, D, B, and Susan. To each of you, thank you.

Thank you also to Cave Canem: Toi Derricotte, Cornelius Eady, and Carolyn Micklem. What a gift.

And thank you to Michael Collier and Bread Loaf, where many of the revisions to this book occurred.

And, of course, my family: Ma and Matty. Thank you.

> . . . *in one hand the rage*
> *I hope you have, in the other the rapture.*
> —Thomas Lux

NEW VOICES

CavanKerry Press is dedicated to springboarding the careers of previously unpublished poets by bringing to print two to three New Voices annually. Manuscripts are selected from open submission; CavanKerry Press does not conduct competitions or charge reading fees.

CavanKerry Press is grateful for the support it receives from the New Jersey State Council on the Arts.

For my father

TABLE OF CONTENTS

FOREWORD

There's something called "working your way into a poet's mind," where you could begin to learn what the poet knows and half understand what he says; and study what he does, how he arranges his thoughts, what his structures are, what are his wondrous comparisons, what words he loves, what are his demons, what he admires, what he constantly returns to, what his vision is—if he should have a vision—who the others are that fill his page, and certainly what he's struggling against and what drove him, like a sledge, into poetry.

I don't mean, say, growing up in Bucks County outside of Philadelphia, or not growing up there or, like Jesus, having a slight limp, or having wings or not, or being great on the court and such—that's merely biography—and anyhow it's the mind's life I'm looking for—biomindus—and its cells and its permutations—for it's out of that life that the poetry comes, the poetry that's valuable, for something anyhow happens anyway to everybody, and it's what you do with it, what you do to it, that counts. As I said, in 1940: "It ain't what you do, it's the way that you do it," though it was F. Oliver and J. Young who wrote it, and Fats and Ella who sang it—or it's what you choose to see; or it's what is forced upon you and how it sings.

What Ross Gay sees, what he sings about, is a crippled woman taking a walk in her wheel chair through the agency of the poet's strong hands; or two brothers embracing in the death chamber, and the untranslatable song between them; or recovery from pain coalescing with the beginning of spring; or the glorious sexy vision of an ankle, or a midriff; or the blue whale's deep sea love scream; or football season in late October. He also sings about the rage and violence inside and the urge to destroy; and the horror of Alzheimer's; and murder; and cancer; and butchered animals and cannibalism; and lynching; and the bullet's journey—almost, almost too neatly the reverse side of the coin, as if one could prove the other—or lived by the other—as if, in the dream of light, he cannot allow himself to forget the darkness, he is so given over to the honest and accurate rendering, or as if he allows himself a final affirmation so long as he admits, or incorporates, the negative.

The affirmation perhaps could too easily be construed as convention, it has in it so much of Emerson, Whitman, and Romantic insistence—even enthusiasm—but I think it's more biblical and is influenced by the extreme views of the prophets and the journey of Jesus. Jeremiah, in the middle of his Laments, where he bemoans the sorrow, and the destruction, can, by a turn of phrase, convert the sorrow into hope and even expectation. The same is true of Isaiah, and others. The religion of Light requires this and I suspect that Gay, like Hart Crane, and Shelley, and Pound is a devotee of that religion, though certainly unconsciously and churchlessly. It would be a stretch maybe, but I would even add the New England presence (called the Reserve) in the American (upper) midwest—where his mother's family originates, just as his father's does in the African American South.

Though I don't want to suggest, in any way, any kind of pat optimism. Gay earns whatever resolution he makes by way of an exhausting struggle with words, ideas, and emotions. I see, at the center of his work, a powerful tension between two forces which I'll call rage and tenderness (or destruction and creation; or violence and love) and it is these two opposing yet complementary forces that create the form, the objective and sustaining mythos, for his poetry, and which gathers into itself those biographical facts which might otherwise be mere fragments of a life, pieces of an existence. The short lyric "Thank You" is an excellent example:

Thank You

If you find yourself half naked
and barefoot in the frosty grass, hearing,
again, the earth's great, sonorous moan that says
you are the air of the now and gone, that says
all you love will turn to dust,
and will meet you there, do not

raise your fist. Do not raise
your small voice against it. And do not
take cover. Instead, curl your toes
into that grass, watch the cloud
ascending from your lips. Walk
through the garden's dormant splendor.
Say only, thank you.
Thank you.

"All you love will turn to dust," and "Say only, thank you./ Thank you."
Or, as in another poem, "Slipping From Lips," he moves from the subway
exhaust pouring up through the steel grates, roasting the homeless men there,
to the joy of "spring's juices" and "a knee pushed into a thigh beneath a break-
fast table."

His is a high diction, and plain-spoken, almost without any irony. Under
other circumstances, such writing could be treacly, but Ross makes it work
through the sheer force of his emotions, the power of his language, his very
belief. It is a joy for me to encounter his ecstatic presence, his faith, his self-
confidence, his rich language. It is a joy, particularly in the face of a certain
dullness that has descended upon American poetry, a dullness consisting var-
iously of pat surrealism, deliberate obscurity, academic cunning, theory-driven
nonsense, mere narration, prose-ache, sing along, language soup and such.
I can't resist reprinting "How to Fall in Love With Your Father," so you will have
the opportunity to read it at least twice. Such love and intelligence, such self-
effacement, such wisdom of form and language is seldom found anywhere in
our poetry.

How to Fall in Love With Your Father

.Put your hands beneath his armpits, bend your knees,
wait for the clasp of his thinning arms; the best lock
cheek to cheek. Move slow. Do not, right now,

recall the shapes he traced yesterday
on your back, moments before being wheeled to surgery.
Do not pretend the anxious calligraphy of touch
was sign beyond some unspeakable animal stammer.
Do not go back further into the landscape of silence you both
tended, with body and breath, until it nearly obscured all
but the genetic gravity between you.

And do not imagine wind now blowing that landscape
into a river which spills into a sea. Because it doesn't.
That's not this love poem. In this love poem
the son trains himself on the task at hand,
which is simple, which is, finally, the only task
he has ever had, which is lifting
the father to his feet.

—Gerald Stern
Lambertville, New Jersey

AGAINST WHICH

ROSS GAY

ONE

Two Bikers Embrace on Broad Street

Maybe, since you're something like me,
you, too, would've nearly driven into oncoming traffic
for gawking at the clutch between the two men
on Broad Street, in front of the hospital,
which would not stop, each man's face
so deeply buried in the other's neck—these men
not, my guess, to be fucked with—squeezing through
that first, porous layer of the body into the heat beneath;
maybe you, too, would've nearly driven over three pedestrians as your head
swiveled to lock on their lock,
their burly fingers squeezing the air from the angels
on the backs of their denim jackets
which reminds you the million and one secrets exchanged
in nearly the last clasp between your father
and his brother, during which the hospital's chatter and rattle
somehow fell silent in deference to the untranslatable
song between them, and just as that clasp endured through
what felt like the gradual lengthening of shadows and the emergence
of once cocooned things, and continues to this day, so, too,
did I float unaware of the 3000 lb machine
in my hands drifting through a stop light while I gawked
at their ceaseless cleave going deeper,
and deeper still, so that Broad Street from Fairmount
to the Parkway reeked of the honey-scented wind
pushed from the hummingbirds now hovering above these two men,
sweetening, somehow, the air until nectar,
yes, nectar gathered at the corners of my mouth like sun-colored spittle,
the steel vehicle now a lost memory
as I joined the fire-breasted birds in listening

to air exchanged between these two men, who are, themselves,
listening, forever, to the muscled contours of the other's neck, all of us
still, and listening, as if we had nothing
to blow up, as if we had nothing to kill.

It Starts at Birth

The newborn railing against the thing behind
the sting of air and light;
against which, too, are castles built, and moats;
against which the futile howl of the body's
trillion cells; against which he will bloody
her nose, often, and she will clasp and kiss
the fists; against which the weight
of lactating breasts, and the gardener's mudpacked
hands, and eyelifts, and the collector of the baby
teeth of his departed children;
against which we put up our hoods and walk
backwards, as if into an icy wind with the appetite
of a river; against which the dazzle
of gold-threaded embroidery inside
the hangman's mask, the perfume
of an ex-lover he sprays beneath the nose hole; against
which the membrane strangling
the general's heart, and the blossom
of blood staining the ballerina's toe-shoes,
and the wet eyes of the dog
whose lungs are muscled
with tumors; against which thousands
of languages, each one broken and blessed
as the last; against which the coil of lovers blent
beneath moonlight, and their sounds: wind
through the trees; against which the ascent
of a crow into the night, a tendril of carrion
dangling in the clutched beak,

and a moment, a diamond
of starlight streaking its black wing,
which is what we, against it, are: impossible,
golden, longing, gone.

Summer

And the sun readies himself for sleep, drowses
backward toward the horizon, and the woods
whisper while the wind massages
the sprawling arms of leaf-thick maples,
heavy shadows cast like dark angels
breast-stroking through the courtyard's grass,
and a man yells to an 8th grade black
kid not to walk around with
white girls, and a sleeveless light blue
shirt flails around his pink chest and pot gut,
and behind him, on the apartment's wall, three
shotguns, and three buildings away the boy's white
mother stirs tomato soup into ground beef
for sloppy joes, and the white girl with the black boy
kicks at the furry clumps of new-mown grass,
stares at her feet, and neighbors whisk the boy
back to his building while the man screams
at the boy, calling him what he does, and kids
play stickball in the tennis courts, and the boy makes
fists in his pockets, and the ice cream truck
slows, passes, and without a word the boy
sits to dinner and lifts the sandwich
to his mouth.

Unclean. Make me.

*And if a woman has an issue, and her issue in her flesh be blood,
she shall be put apart seven days. And if any man lie with her at
all, and her flowers be upon him, he shall be unclean seven days.*

Leviticus, Chapter 15

When the body blooms, you must
put your face to it. Lay tongue
to the lathe, the blessed
lather. Song like marble spun
into silk. The human
loom. The thread limning your lips. Breathe
there. Fill your lungs
with birth's florid shadow. This is the common dream of the living
and dead: to not only meet
the maker, but to taste its sweet. Even God
should know this.

Alzheimer's

She stood in her doorway, asked my name
again- something she would never
remember. A breeze
loosed some cherry blossoms, petals
flipping through her open arms
as she whispered, *Look what God has done,*
look what God
has done.

Broken Mania

This is not a joke
when I wrap my hand tight
around the drunk man's throat,
the drunk who heaves his girlfriend
around the Chevy, while she begs
no and please and the pub's other drunk men
won't be bothered because the Flyers play
the Red Wings in game 2 for the cup.
This, Drunk Man, is not a joke, and when
I left my pal's house for some hot tea
at 7-11 I did not know that we would meet,
but meet we did, intimates we have become, I would say,
what with that gurgling noise slurping
about in your throat. And your girlfriend clutches my
arm, wide-eyed and sad, not sure for whom
she roots, but she knows her duty, where
she sleeps. This is not a joke,
Drunk Man. If the time and place
were right, you would have been dead, your tongue
yanked out and nailed to your forehead, but the time
was not right, bouncers tore me from you,
and I was wearing bear slippers, big, furry,
with soft claws. Maybe
I was too self-conscious to finish the job.
Maybe it was my friend at my side,
just released from a funny farm for a psychotic
episode, whispering and quaking, *That's enough,*
that's enough. You did not
know this about me, or my friend, did not

know the previous day his hand dug
hard into my shoulder from the car's back
seat as we approached another hospital, pleading,
Please don't let them
do this to me. Don't do
this to me. That he hasn't
slept in five days and is wired, told me
things I can't repeat for fear of my tongue
turning black rot and infecting my brain,
that it has nothing to do with samaritinism, the woman,
or humanity, this Drunk Man, is about me,
about me shrinking your universe
around your throat like a noose, showing you that
to you, at this second, I am God,
and until my friend's mania is broke
my arm melts rocks and is a machine
for murder.

Slipping From Lips

The gingko trees leaning outside my window
one month ago a blazed gold now sulk
like the withered talons of a thousand dead
and decaying birds, and the subway's smog
roasts homeless men through the clenched teeth
of steel grates, and the afternoon shadows stretch and pull,
the sun's lounge now long, and god, I'm happy,
happy for the crystal tipped lips of frost bitten grass,
happy for my throat's slight, raspy burn, and the death
of another year, hungry for the birth of the new,
for the tiny streams weeping from the soot-blackened
and gravel thick snows piled like filthy diamonds
against the curb, hungry for the river's clay banks
to shake free the jagged ice, hungry
for the first sun-splashed neck's swanny curve,
like the bent stream of light-pierced honey
drooling off the mason jar's mouth, hungry
for the first pick-up holler hanging on the basketball courts,
the stinging ping of balls singing each to each,
and the cum trees, and honeysuckle, and the rotting
garbage cooked in the dumpsters, when the first step
out of the house douses you so thick in spring's juices,
when there's no escaping it, everything touched-
knuckles dragged across a bare wrist,
a knee pushed into a thigh beneath a breakfast table,
the whispered tickle of wind slipping from lips-
is scented, dripping, and wet.

Poem Beginning With a Line Overheard in the Gym

I'd drive a thousand miles to suck the dick
of the man who fucked her once. If you're like
me, the pristine lilt of iambic verse will halt
your dumb work on the bench press. You also love

the hyperbolic rattling of logic's cage.
Mostly, you love the way the loins fuel
the tongue's conjure. But what grand sadness dragged
in misplaced desire; as though from another's memory

of smoke·we might glean some end
of ache. Truth be told, ache's shop is long
set up. Is birth's phantom limb. Let's, instead, admire
the tether. Its blue flame. Its

wrangle with the loamy earth for the body,
the keepsake.

The Hernia

The gingko bones shiver a bit, dream
of full bloom, of a million fan-shaped leaves
and a million juicy stink bombs. This year
I'll watch those buds push out of the trees'
knuckles, I'll watch the coat of green slowly
fill the wiry limbs; each night I'll see
less wood, more elegant foliage- it won't
sneak up on me like last year, one day
so cold the car coughs and spits, the next
so warm Kennedy Boulevard oozes with open-toed
shoes, with, God-bless them, those Jersey
City dresses, cotton butterflies riding
and hiding the saunter's supple, muscled crux;
I'll feel the warmth slither out of winter's linger
like a python pulling out of a withered cloak of scales,
I'll finger the pink, sutured worm crawling into my
navel, walk to the courts, careful not to
sneeze, I'll watch the first golden river
of ballers hollering back and forth, hear
that perfect sound, the rock's pound and bounce,
and I'll fall in love 14 times in one evening,
once with a good head fake, once a crossover, maybe
a good head of cornrows, or a woman's quick
walk outside the fence, trying to be invisible
to the twenty sweaty black men on the sideline.
I'll be waiting, you see, for the repaired
leak in my belly's lining to heal.
Doctor says four weeks from surgery: May 1st.
That's four weeks beginning of spring, four

weeks when the jaunt to the court is a sugar
soaked breast stroke to a Darwinian black top
mambo where swap-dog-kin swim
like a five-finned fish, like a fist wet with the sweat of sex—
let's face it; I love you,
and for one month, starting tomorrow,
my heart, for you, will thrash itself like a horsefly
caught in a thimble, and I'll be that kid, you know
him, sad-eyed and palms a'glisten, fogging
the aquarium glass, begging the ray's smooth wings
to cast a gray, fluid shadow across his back,
the water's gentle pull and push the truest soothe
he could imagine, except I'm dreaming of a drop
step, a fast break, a no-look pass, and God, I hope
you wait for me (as I will for you); and as the syrupy
drugs roll through my veins, and the one hour
undertow takes hold, I'll be thinking
of you, angel, the only one who loves me
exactly as I want: silently
and in my dreams.

The Truth

Because he was 38, because this
was his second job, because
he had two daughters, because his hands
looked like my father's, because at 7
he would walk to the furniture warehouse,
unload trucks 'til 3 AM, because I
was fourteen and training him, because he made
$3.75 an hour, because he had a wife
to look in the face, because
he acted like he respected me,
because he was sick and would not call out
I didn't blink when the water
dropped from his nose
into the onion's perfectly circular
mouth on the Whopper Jr.
I coached him through preparing.
I did not blink.
Tell me this didn't happen.
I dare you.

Man Tries to Commit Suicide With a Crossbow

for Thomas Lux

And fails. First, imagine the weapon
pointing heavenward beneath his chin. After the trigger's
quick tick, the following: what, for said
undead, must have sounded like a rocket's stratospheric crash,
which is to say the arrow just
crested the crown (i.e. it got stuck). At which point, the head
now a kebob, said undead had
the wherewithal to unscrew the skewer
from the little lodged missile and pull it out. To walk
to the emergency room.

I love to think
grace takes strange shapes: the arrow
balm to the howl of neurons.
To think of that walk beneath the velvet night.
Stay with me. Don't think
headache. Think
instead: the stars' ancient light warming
his just budding horn.

Coming Out of You

The gasp and tender slackening of your jaw,
like a wake in black waters, they say,
should make me see the vast
and vacuous night as a singular
burden no blend can bliss,
which is to say, they say, no
union defies Big Daddy Time's pungent
and undulous, double-sided sword
upon which is inscribed (in our own script, they say!)
our every weightless name. They say
when the bloodbath comes
the only hand you hold is your own, they say
that gasp is a candle
unto the long and dis-threading dark.
They say this
and they say that.
But they've not been instructed
by moonlight choiring in your low
back's glaze of sweat, nor felt
your voice as silk kissing
my skull's quiet innards, nor seen all time
wisped into this thoracic glance,
this needle's eye, this gasp
of me leaving you
and us becoming the imperturbable
breath of the undead.

Angels Out of Reach

That winter I threw back shots of rum
until my throat's smooth tissue
grew hot as a desert's sunbleached sands, until
each hour was spent chasing the slow hum
at the neck's base, and God, I can only recall the sun sinking,
recall the thick, cold nights leaning heavy on my lungs,
remember the season's first blizzard and a drunk pal stumbling
into a head-high drift and leaving a six-foot shadow-filled snow angel,
remember a woman in my apartment, first seeing her calf's elegant descent
to her ankle, the shard of midriff gleaming beneath her tank top,
I'll never forget it, her long body leaning into the doorjamb,
that smile sharp and subtle as clear glass drifting at a sandy lake bottom,
and two weeks later her telling me of being raped,
of the booze and sweaty dick and her wrists' bruises,
and didn't I work harder at my own death and dream
just as hard of murder, and didn't I commend the
the clear plastic rum-filled bottle for caressing
me closer to tears, didn't I drink until my heart and brain
nearly crossed paths like a fire-lit keg of ammonia and bleach,
and didn't I clutch the flimsy bottle's neck while gagging down
the dried and bitter mushrooms, while trudging through the season's
second blizzard, while I climbed a tree to more closely feel
the frigid breath from the earth's icy lungs, the wind more a cold
dry punch in the throat than anything else, and didn't the brittle
branches sprawl like trillions of capillaries sauntering
the brain's slick folds, and didn't I sit roosted
in that tree for hours, and didn't the wind whip

so quick the snow never quite reached the ground,
and wasn't the snow beneath the streetlights
like the Milky Way's swirl
of angels dancing out of reach?

Let Me Be

after Philip Levine

Like a one-armed boomerang
whistling through a typhoon's eye,
a steamship's blind plow
through miles of coal black, star-flecked sea,
like the swollen river's stubborn chew through
tons of stone, cars and trees tiny
floating buoys on my shoulders,
time enough and every thing
worn to silty dust, I'm a god-damned
krill-bearded blue whale howling a deep
sea love scream, you see, I'm a spaceship
singing through a star's stinging
heat shroud, its fire gown, my heart
so fat and hot every passing thing joy-singed
with this overripe, honey-
stuffed, juggernaut sweetness; let me
be back to your sunlight lined lips,
your muscled hands, your morning eye's
first opening, let me be a glint
of sundust drifting down your windpipe's
glisten, lodging in your red wet
bloodpump's silken clench, that ruby
smooth muscle's every move, let me be,
let me be.

Dial

Was the wet scent of Dial
threw me back into the showers'
crowd, bruised herds of men,
muddied, blood-stained some,
many limping on racked and aching
legs, the raspy water clap
smacking the cement floor, some
still boys, 3 hours full-tilt and still
lithe and spry, arms and legs less
dented, hips less crooked, but most
of us more like Ace, defensive back,
our headhunter, whose arthritic scapula
and rotator cuffs would never allow him to
raise his hands above his head. Wizened
and tired, labor camp whores whose
degree (those who got it) was the fee.
Would be with this battered crew
of mostly violent, mostly kind, half
sick kin where I learned,
believe this, how men might love
each other. This from rapists,
saints, attempted murderers, bankers,
teachers, drug dealers, and at least
two suicides—one who wrote
poems, hung; and one who drove
his jeep full speed at a semi, and when
just half shook, crawled from the wreck,
leapt in front of the next—who

must've looked something like an angel
to that trucker, flying west
for what seemed
a long time.

Pulled Over in Short Hills, NJ, 8:00 AM

It's the shivering. When rage grows
hot as an army of red ants and forces
the mind to quiet the body, the quakes
emerge, sometimes just the knees,
but, at worst, through the hips, chest, neck,
until, like a virus, slipping inside the lungs
and pulse, every ounce of strength tapped
to squeeze words from my taut lips,
his eyes scanning my car's insides, my eyes,
my license, and as I answer the questions
3, 4, 5 times, my jaw tight as a vice,
his hand massaging the gun butt, I
imagine things I don't want to
and inside beg this to end
before the shiver catches my
hands, and he sees,
and something happens.

Leaving New Orleans

I'm leaving a city where the living and dead mix,
where the dank summer air's reek is more ghost
than any town needs. The plane knifing through
night. I met someone here whose eyes drip
with the scars of some slaughter, the echo
whispering, There is pain you can't even begin
to know. And 33,000 feet down, a human galaxy's
mute burn.

The Heaven

This is the Heaven: pigshit, tulips, a filthy child
whose eyes are wide enough to bleed. And his four siblings,
each hungry as him. Maybe, probably, one will die
from some disease that twists the air
from his lungs. It will hurt. The Heaven
is pain inside and out. And love
thick as ore. The Heaven
takes and takes, smirks; is the weight sinking a burlap sack
of kittens. The light warming
the silent wake. The mother.
A backyard thick with bones.
Plunge a thumb in the soil: blood. And
teeth. Song like shrapnel.
The Heaven is this
and more. Sun glancing off the gunwales' backs.
And the vulture's wait. The creases
in a man's face when he enters into prayer. The way
his words turn into a shroud of light.
A conversation between a man and an idea
I can almost see. I can almost
believe.

TWO

The Voice
for Gerald Stern

It's there, on your walk to breakfast,
from Lombard to Fitzwater, down 10th
to avoid the projects, the bony trees'
wicked creak and sway, the air a crisp lick
to your cheek and neck, it's there, in the waitress's
eyes, it's there in your gut, burning,
burning, the coal, he called it, we are at its
mercy, he said, he who taught you
how to wear tenderness like a shawl,
or a fedora, who taught you a splayed
heart worn like a rhino-sized pendant,
who taught you cursing and elegance,
and shouting, it's there, in your father's
hunched back, his exhausted gait, his hiding,
a burning, yes, a burning, not
tears, they've burnt up years back,
but a rage, and a violence, a need
to murder, and exalt, even your body
built for the task, hands long and strong
for strangling, or prayer, the road crumbling
behind you, no turning back, you're locked,
and you spit molten ore each day, each blessed
day you glow, you blaze, you burn, you
raze, each day you crack open a rock hard cataract,
you see, for once, one new goddamned thing, you
see, you fill your lungs, and you scream, and you
scream, and you scream.

Ruptured Aneurysm

If there is a history, and I think there is, I do not
think I own it. Watch its billowed white sail
and gnarled mast rocking toward the horizon,
one see-through slip-knot tethering our every neck
to the hull's gut. Watch that ship's indifferent
plod slice, instead, the widening pool of blood bubbling
a lullaby from the torn grin of flesh glistening beneath
a landowner's chin, and above him, boots wet with that spill's
sprawl, a man who whittled from a throat a window
through which to imagine something like
a future. Look at the wakes in the crimson lake roll
with the same crush as the sea's unfurling exhalations,
the ship's course still steady, and constant, the keel now
warted and scarred with the stringy growth of barnacles,
look closely, until you see the thrust of blood
leaning its persistent shoulder through a rip in my aunt's
artery, until you know her intuition to tell me this story,
the story of her father, a share-cropper killing
the man who stood between himself and Cincinnati, and know,
as you do, that if she dies, swallowing this story,
she becomes little more than a frayed string in the braid
of that ship's rope, limp and mute
in the arms of the night sky's
long dead light.

Marionette

for Amadou Diallo

The few strings snap and pull
the doll's flimsy limbs for his last
ballet, an American piece, arms flung
like a flamingo's wings, his sashay
a flame's undulation, dip, wave, head
snapped into a skygaze, a pained grin white
beneath the doorway's light, legs braiding
in the climactic pirouette, convulsive
shoulders rolling, the body's final drift
smooth as a sun-baked bloodflake
flecked off a rhino's horn, the gored
corpse sweet meat to a smoky gauze
of ravenous flies humming and blood-
sucking tiny gunpowder-singed hearts,
charred kiss marks, until, at last,
the strings go slack, the doll
sprawls in a crippled collapse, his face
half lit, the puppeteers praising this black
ghost's steel-pierced, last dying
quake, the deed sweet and clean,
and that last wheeze, an escaping, you've heard
it, drops the floodgates for the real ghosts,
a bouquet of them, a blitzkrieg of black orchids
roaring. And they blaze.

One Eye Gone Black

You knew the cancer would grow
over both lungs, make them
black, mossy shadows. But no one
told you about the blindness.
That before your breathing sounded
curdled and raw, one eye
would phase out, the morbid
meandering, a slow go, making
your chest ache like a tractor
breaking through bone.
The last time I visited you, 110
lbs, one eye's sight gone black
and your arm's keloid approaching
the bicep in size, you gave the same
mechanic's vice-grip handshake, a challenge
and warning that your killing
would not be easy.

Bar-b-q

On 60 Minutes
a man explained that as a secret
police official in South Africa he once,
to make a body
that he had killed disappear, roasted it.
He and his associates at the same time
eating bar-b-q
while the man sizzled.
I never would have figured that
as a way to dispose of a body.
More the traditional, club skull
to pulp with gun butts or baseball bats
and bury it in the woods.
But roasting. Think of that,
the smell of human, cooking,
though certainly not much different
than swine, intermingling, tainting
the smell and taste of the grilled
chicken sandwiches and ale. Olfactory
makes up at least half
of your taste sensation. Eating
the killed and dead.
The spit sunk in the dead
man's ass, probed
through the mouth, locked
like some devil's horn, the fat
drip drip from the meaty parts.

Hams, ribs. A face
emptied of skin, eyes,
person.

These men went free.

But you can see in their eyes,
weaker than the dead, these men
are dying by the second.
By the second.
Sustained by the killing.

Teeth smoked black through that screamed smile.

Song of the Pig Who Gave the Poet, Age 3, Worms

You did not know what the hands
that held your hands would do
to me, my mother, and siblings. You couldn't
imagine it. And so,
instead of escaping your clutch
and snuggle, I waited, threw my tiny
hooves in the air, gave you my belly.
The other hogs watched.
Although I dreamt of opening your throat
with the same blade stained
with the blood of my kin, your touch
felt good, honest, kissing my snout and eyes,
my pig's mouth. And when you left
(walking backward, weren't you?), I knew
I had marked you, your little mouth, mouth
that kissed me, whispered in my ears,
that spoke to no one about the mud
and shit caked in my hooves,
that screamed with joy at the sight of
pigs, that loved the taste
of bacon and ham, and pork chops
most of all—for the lies and smiles,
and for your dull memory (do you
recall the color of my eyes, the speckles
of pink crawling across my snout, the smell
of the smooth ridge of my spine?), for this especially,
I tried to mark you with the pain of worms, which,
like everything else, failed: hands, snout,
windblown sand of our bones.

Gophers

are ugly. Fat teeth thrust from the mouth,
gnarled and wet, hungry for alfalfa
or a finger. Insolent fellas,
their blind squint filled with such distaste.
But that is not why we kill them.
Gophers plow subway tunnels
beneath crops, mounds
of tractor mangling dirt lumping
the farmer's field. Farmers pay a buck-fifty
a pair for the front feet. Township pays a buck
for the rears and tail.
And how do we kill them?
Two ways. The death-trap
and the pan-trap. The former, more humane,
actually, looks like a gaped cobra's mouth,
and when sprung, clamps sharp prongs
around or through the gopher's gut.
The pan-trap, on the other hand, clamps
an ankle, the gopher pissed off and frothing
when you pull him, clawing the air like a bridge
jumper, from his hole, and lay him
on the pick-up truck's rusty gate, smashing
his head to pieces with a blood-flecked hammer.
The smell of manure sweet and light in the air,
Grampa winks,
snips the gopher's feet and tail,
and you toss the limp,
limbless thing in a sack, happy
for this, one of the things
you're really good at.

The Rearing Back

Warted lumps of pulpy flesh, pure jump
and piss, rainbathing, had-been dry backs
drinking the night's wet. Hop hop. The supple
skin, even on this broken asphalt

the dream of scumtopped ponds, the legless emerge,
the current's breath coaxing their blend. And the boy,
scooping up two or three. And the stone wall.
And the low sky still. The rearing back. The throw.

Beat Him Again

Ubiquitous pip of spit licked to the twisted lip,
this, plus the half-pimp half-gimp hitch in his stroll
made plain his break and deform: weakness the ripe smell
of blood. Tourette's was a foreign word

to kids whose dads smelled bad after work. Look,
his tongue was broke as an incontinent dog. It
would slip. To us that meant beat him. What else?
Beat him again.

Love's Burn Needs

Some of our big kids might snatch you
in the night, press your ear and cheek
to the concrete, and place a cigarette's glow end
an inch from your eye. And a dad like mine

might crease that same night like fire
lights a dry field. Some love's burn needs
the warm breeze of fear. These boys got tamed. My hand
shaking inside the man's shaking hand the quick walk home.

Postcard: Lynching of an Unidentified Man, circa 1920

after Lucille Clifton

It's not his imperceptible sway, or the whine
of the rope's braid straining against his weight,
or his right pant leg shoved above his shin; it's not
the wide blade of light slicing the snapshot, behind
the body, or through him, depending on your
angle, it's not the way his still-tucked white
shirt becomes that light, becomes the source of that light,
not the way the dead fist inside his chest
becomes the source of that light; it's not the way
everyone save him
looks at the camera, poses—
one young man, nearly handsome, pushing
the hanged body so he might fit more snug
into the frame—or the way an adult turns a child
toward the camera
as if to say, *stand still so they can see*
what we've done; it's not the neck's torque and bulge
or the skin's color—

       it's the angle of his head, its impossible,
owlish twist toward something only he can see, or away
from something only he can see, it's as though
the same flash that makes the dumb-looking boy grin,
to the hanged man
it burns.

The Whisper

Not a roar. Not
cyclones of flies
rasping thorny legs against
a ditch of bulldozed dead.
Not the drift and bob
of a limp head or arm
pushing through a river's tumble. Not
the last wet gasp
of the fetus ripped
from its shot mother's belly
and shot. This is bone
dust with a mica shine.
This is a three-legged dog's
crippled skip beneath the teeth
of a sleet storm. This is sand,
mudflakes, skin and hair
packing black the floorboard's
cracks, and the scrape,
the scrape and moan, you
can barely hear it, of the people
on whom the house is built.

For a Young Emergency Room Doctor

Although this prayer should first dress
the dead boy's wounds,
nine gunshots, in and out, the spine pierced
and wrecked enough to twist
the head's dangle
backward; and before the body,
the night through which the bullets chewed;
and the latex sheathing the hands of the cops who
dragged and dropped
the boy on the gurney-
last touch of this world
gloved; and the heart's dirge,
dwindling lament
for spilled blood, lost love; too, for the blankets of light
wrapping him, jewelling
the viscous liquid slicking his lips:

it's for the living. For those
who close the boy's eyes again
and again. For whom
salve is the wound's mend, the eased bleed.
Who tell the story
while eating. Who, too, die
at the dying's rising pile.

Cousin Drowses on the Flight to Kuwait

Does she dream of Saturn of molars
of the jeweled corridors of palaces dream
the commander's robes
his crooked smile dream
sooty bellows of cumulous
dream dress dream a lover's breath dream
wind over dunes the voices
riding night winds dream whispered
light of stars dream teddy bear dream mother
father dream baby
sister dream mirages
dream your body riding the air
dream the body's tenuous earthen cleave dream
birthmark or crooked toe
dream every hair on your head dream
galaxies aswirl at each finger's tip
the trigger's smooth tick
dream brown faces your
brown face dream the commander
cockeyed the tumble of diamonds stumbling
from his toothless mouth
his florid robes flailing above a fat body
dream the dragon's toothpick
fibula femur dream orchard abloom
in bloody soil dream
the improbability of your legs
ambulatory pleasures
sand frosty towpath gravel
road dream breezes combing

clover growth threading a graveyard's grass
dream the random calculus of shrapnel
or your skin wrapping the chorale of muscle
and bone the galactic swell
of blood cells heaving
breathe dream
breathe

The Bullet, in Its Hunger

The bullet, in its hunger, craves the womb
of the body. The warm thrum there. Begs always
release from the chilly, dumb chamber.
Look at this one whose glee
at escape was outshone only by the heavens
above him. The night's even-keeled
breath. All things thus far dreams from
his cramped bunker. But now
the world. Let me be a ravenous diamond
in it, he thinks, chewing through the milky jawbone
of this handsome seventeen-year-old. Of course
he would have loved to nestle amidst the brain's
scintillint catacombs (which, only for the boy's dumb luck,
slipped away) but this will do. The bullet does
not, as the boy goes into shock, or as his best friend
stutters, palming the fluid wound, want to know the nature
of the conflict, nor the sound of the shooter's
mother in prayer, nor the shot child's future harmonies:
the tracheostomy's muffled wheeze
threaded through the pencil's whisper as the boy scrawls *I'm
scared*. No.
The bullet, like you, simply craves
the warmth of the body. Like you, only wants
to die in someone's arms.

Litany

say birdsong
at death's bed-
side plus honeybees
their hover and thirst say
thickets of clover
aquiver the gold
swell limning
morning clouds
the light behind it
say wet eyes
the orb's cock-eyed swirl
extubate
say the honey
between nape and scapula
a slow ride
between two points
the plush rug of ivy
swallowing this tree
pissing
in a wood say
the last rattle of the thorax
the peristaltic earth
say home say

THREE

The First Breath

This is the landscape I could live for. Endless
rows of snowdusted fields, the frozen juts
of chopped cornstalks craning their necks
to a thaw. This midwest is not mine—not
the silos butting against a graying and slumped
sky or the high-tension wires
threading acres of soybeans or the dumb sheep
standing knee-deep in slush. This belongs
to the folks of mine who made a life massaging
from the earth enough to feed a family, and some
pigs, enough to post two headstones in nearly
that same earth: one of whom has become that earth,
and the other who wishes as much. It's a cold
winter out here. Everything left standing wishes
it had gone to sleep in the fall; even the trees
will laugh and spit when you promise them
a spring and soil worth drinking from. But the old man,
he knows better, he's been at it all his life. He can sense a thaw
around the corner, a sort of quiet opening,
he's always thought. And if you see him sitting in his
rocker, eyeing the slumped pine-branches burning
off their frozen burden, you'll notice that he's already
gone down into that earth, dreaming
of the first breath of soil.

How To Fall in Love With Your Father

Put your hands beneath his armpits, bend your knees,
wait for the clasp of his thinning arms; the best lock
cheek to cheek. Move slow. Do not, right now,

recall the shapes he traced yesterday
on your back, moments before being wheeled to surgery.
Do not pretend the anxious calligraphy of touch
was sign beyond some unspeakable animal stammer. Do not

go back further into the landscape of silence you both
tended, with body and breath, until it nearly obscured all
but the genetic gravity between you.

And do not imagine wind now blowing that landscape
into a river which spills into a sea. Because it doesn't.
That's not this love poem. In this love poem
the son trains himself on the task at hand,
which is simple, which is, finally, the only task
he has ever had, which is lifting
the father to his feet.

1,2

'Dying Is An Art'
Sylvia Plath

Not really. Save the song
the sickle sings, we expire the same: lights out.
But what of the florid burden of living?
This one's body craves
the bottomless caesura. Just ask his bone marrow
belting out its omnivorous hymn.
But the man's not just a gumbo
of muscle and bones.
He'll swim through a bog of poison
to stay on with it.
Leave the better part of most meals,
give or take an innard, swimming
in the john. And when his pimpled thighs beg
reprieve from needle pricks,
he will ask his pal to pinch and pierce the as-yet-untouched triceps.
To stay on with it.
Catch my drift? Dying's a lowly knock-off
of the real thing: the man
who, on erasure's edge, spears with his hands this earth,
shoves the muddy stuff in his mouth,
and chews.

Late October in Easton
for Derek Mast

We watched the men shoot hoops, two ex-pros
in them, a Knick and a Buck, agile dinosaurs
sauntering through the gleam off the court's back.
We watched the ex-Knick turn for a rebound,
crumple to the ground, six feet ten inches of man
sprawled through the paint, an arm flung, palm up,
across the baseline. We watched his son
sprint to his side, press the carotid, tuck his ear
close to his dad's parted, still lips, watched those thick hands,
clasped into one, attack the heart like John Henry's massive sledge,
pushing at his dad's fat heart, the thing moaning
its last violent lament in that castle,
that huge rib cage, all the bone pillars pointing to Heaven.
And didn't the son try like mad to make the heart sing,
didn't he massage the smooth tissue of his father's heart
like a miner sifting through sand for gold?
And didn't the father's last exhalation crawl
from his throat, the eyes locked vacant on the court's lights,
that raspy sigh, the sound of breeze-blown leaves, almost
like a hand on the son's brow, almost the father saying,
It's ok. It's done.

The next day, a mile away, the Delaware still rolled drowsy
through the hills, and it was football season, late October,
the miles of corn surrounding our field had come down,
letting the fall wind press itself against my face, I can smell it,
the wind getting its bite from the river, and I remember standing
on the free bridge after practice, at five o'clock, when the sun slipped back

into the horizon's black sleeve, I remember
the orange and gold glow of the forest
hanging on the river's rippled shoulders,
and the way that river, silent and alone,
was always going home.

Outside The Wake of a Friend's Father

Although I know I should be trying hard to palpate
this common sorrow, to unspool sympathy
for the bereaved stumbling and sobbing
inside those doors, my tongue sits like a stone
in my mouth and the truth's matter is
I am, right now, contemplating the mysteries of light
on an ankle, that one in particular, which,
beneath this sun, favors the earth's lush shapes from an airplane,
and it might be the dogwood abloom
like a gaggle of screaming angels
makes me dumb or the wrenched gut's slight of hand
but that ankle has put death to bed
and has me dreaming of the lucky saint whose tongue transcribes channeled
          Sapphic fragments throughout the minute ravines there,
and I know I should stop
except I hear my own father's dust, at this moment, whispering in a breeze,
          no, no, go on,
so let me sing the largest
praise upon the subtlest juncture of flesh and bone,
bony bud the pillow upon which scripture was dreamt
and writ, mother of the muses and their gowns
flowing just above their ankles,
and the sun's hot mouth breathing on me in dress pants afraid to enter the
          parlor for my own wound lying in that casket
rubs also its lips along that miniscule mountain
of motility, crossroads
of the foot's baroque architecture
and the girder of the shin, delicate crux
culling at once birdsong and the melodious stirrings of worms,

ecstatic axis whose dragonfly-like skimming of this New Jersey asphalt
    parking lot sucks gasps and moans from all of Trinidad's tarpits,
    ankle,
ankle, for which I would give my good hand to listen
to its trillion vascular secrets, which include heartbreak's 4268
glistening names: silk, stamen, inseam, moonlight,
diamond, father, smoke, mirage, ankle,
don't ask, just close your eyes,
get on your knees,
and pray.

The Drive

This was one of those nights,
the radio off, only the wind's hum
squeezing through the broken
window, a near-perfect happiness
driving over Rt. 611's elegant, unlit
bends, the road nestling the river,
stopping for rest at a hotel in Easton. Tomorrow
the sun's tongue will lie across the glass back
of the Delaware like a white sword, and I'll wake
happy, some fears cast off, I'll sing,
I bet, think of a woman's gait like a seaweed
strand in a stream's breeze, I'll touch my
chest, feel the young bulldozer's pounding howl,
I'll be happy, despite my best friend's crude hands
endlessly folded in drink, I'll be happy
despite his exhaustion, and thorough
as it is, the windblown reeds in our childhood's
caustic woods still sway, and the dingy creek's
slow drag still pulls silt over salamanders,
and the crane's muddy stilt still slips
from the water, the circle of tiny breaking
wakes oscillating to the creek's banks, until,
for an instant, the bird's white wings swallow
the sun, for one second the thing
caught like a splayed angel, an ivory flame,
and with one swift pull, a broad heft, it leaves,
and the light, despite you, or me,
or any love or suffering between us,
the sweet, sweet light,
it's blinding.

The Poet Dreams of His Father

who is naked, and stretching
his hip flexors,
who is yogic, in fact,
as a phantom
string pulls the top of his bald head straight
into heaven. Sinking
into this posture, he tells me to rub his flanks,
which I do.

It's safe to assume
the father didn't see this return coming. Maybe
he'd twist back as cologned wind or light
dappling a steeple of trees.
Or entering dreams, he'd whisper
something about the gold ribbon spinning through

    shadows,
leave us clutching the warmth.

But look closely. The body
(see the tell-tale scar zipping
the hip, the second toes' broken necks) is the poet's.
    The poet's
as much as the father's. Which is to say, breath
braided to air. The distance
between us. Dust
on the tip of my tongue.

Why Would We Not

for my cousin, Patrick Rosal

Why would we not speak to the dead
who have in their union with the womb of the sea and earth
become the hands caressing the burdened muscle's churn
what dumb fist said and when did it say
do not chew bone silt
for the sweet there
which as silky loam becomes pure as the idea of air
said do not study the precise composition of your hands
to speak to your father said do not
clutch the scent of a food from a galaxy of islands
and be reminded your mother's blowsy back
as she studies oil in a pan
said do not speak to your dead
in this season roadside flora rapt and the river beside me
smoothing stones cast in the same breath as the cosmos who said
this rain to prime the lusty pump of spring do not
speak to the dead who at long last listen to lament and prayer
at last have become the fullest proportions of light
and long for little more than the overt confession
the wound's flooding the crime for which
we are forgiven
who said, cousin, we ought not speak to our dead
who have moved into the threnody of our body's wet machinery
your mother my father
kin in the folds of everywhere
which is this deep breath I take
now to swear the oncoming salve of light

promised me by the earth's temporary flirtation with the sun
to you father I speak and sing and cry
and curse and tell you the next gorgeous thing I see
which is now

The Cleave

The ache you speak of feeling
when you leave your sleeping child, let
it swell into a wail ageless as the wind
spit from wavebreaks, feel it in the baby's
milky breath and gaze that gazes past even
you, that weave of grief and rapture,
the ceaseless cleave, the please,
don't leave.

Dead Hair

Let's be frank; this is hard work. Not just the deaf and stiff
clients, but the ways they get here. You know
this. You know some skulls get scarred before and after
the drift. You know ceremony's sad magic is a windblown
veil over this rigid fact.

But to her, little worry. Fit the wig right. Broaden
the braid. Maybe a hat for the calm passage. And if
the undertaker's a man, assist him with her body's
last show. The bust, mostly. She'd thank you.

If I know her right, she's talking to the corpse,
its new name *Baby*. You might think the work
dead-end, a kind of parade for worms. You're wrong.
Her comb's divining a ravenous choir of light. It builds
a beauty for the beauty the body
will meet.

Library Quiet Room

If your dense work keeps your head smashed
to the grindstone, or if your back faces them,
you will not know the cause of the earthy moans
and chirps behind you in the library's quiet room. Until
in a reflection you see, like flirting
hummingbirds, the hand ballet of the deaf,
who do not hear the noises
they make: love
grunts, the drones of sleep, mostly
the racket of wonder.
Close your eyes; somehow
this knobby sonic landscape makes perfect sense. You wish
they could hear it too.

The Walk

What do you say
when a woman asks to take
a walk, but she's crippled, and
the walk is you walking
behind her, gripping the wheelchair's
handles so tight if they had human
hands you'd have snapped every tiny
one, and this woman with a sorrow
you've never seen before, even her neck
and thick hands are heavy with it, what do
you say when your legs, battered
from years of sport, are blessed and strong
as any animal your size; what do you
say when a woman's smile carries in it
every impossibility, every barefoot stroll
through hay, every game of hopscotch;
what do you say when her husband is too
tired to carry her down the embankment
to the river, the one place in this world
where her limp legs lift to the moonlit
surface like dolphins teasing gravity, when,
despite your own clumsy inclination
toward despair, you have never been so
happy, maybe because you finally know
in this life there is not time for heroes and angels,
just the chance to warm with your hands something
that will touch someone else, so you
smile, and you say,
Yes, let's walk.

Her Breath

Wasn't she in that midnight moon,
so wide, each beam an arm of light
whitening the canyon wall's spiny lines,
her opaque stare a luminous vision
of those elusive heart-shredding joys,
millions of them, like steam
smoking from rain-splashed August asphalt; you
know them: her voice, her breath, the smell of the god-sent
crook between her chin and neck, all so much
the glint across the canyon's vast gape, miles
away that tiny fire's windblown blade casting light
on all we have, which is nothing, nothing at all,
except that which we love.

Outbreath

I had been dying a long time,
boy. Do you ever remember me
not dragging this broken sack
of slag and ash? Summer picnics in shorts,
shirts off, ever remember my body
not threaded with kiloys?
I've watched people, in bodies I'd die for,
die; knees, hips, ankles all free
of steel, free of ache. I guess my blessing
was the strange, near painless
cancer that just closed down shop, darkened
the lights even on that stupid, tireless
heart, worker who swore that with belief
alone, with love of blood alone, he
might save this body despite
the mind's dirge for the long sleep.
            And then I slept. Just like that. And
I stopped hearing that crippled thing behind me.
The rattle and wheeze. It just stopped,
like an outbreath. And after? The sound of wind
inside a wind.

Patience

You wait. You wait until
his sweats won't stop.
Until papery skin just cloaks
each clavicle,
until the necrotic tumor's sloughing
keeps the gut taut with fluid.
You wait dry heaves and wet, wait the man's
last recede to notice the freckles
sprinkled across his nose and cheeks.
To put your lips to them.
Each one.

Thank You

If you find yourself half naked
and barefoot in the frosty grass, hearing,
again, the earth's great, sonorous moan that says
you are the air of the now and gone, that says
all you love will turn to dust,
and will meet you there, do not
raise your fist. Do not raise
your small voice against it. And do not
take cover. Instead, curl your toes
into the grass, watch the cloud
ascending from your lips. Walk
through the garden's dormant splendor.
Say only, thank you.
Thank you.

CAVANKERRY'S MISSION

Through publishing and programming, CavanKerry Press connects communities of writers with communities of readers. We publish poetry that reaches from the page to include the reader, by the finest new and established contemporary writers. Our programming brings our books and our poets to people where they live, cultivating new audiences and nourishing established ones.

OTHER BOOKS IN THE NEW VOICES SERIES

Howard Levy, *A Day This Lit*
Karen Chase, *Kazimierz Square*
Peggy Penn, *So Close*
Sondra Gash, *Silk Elegy*
Sherry Fairchok, *Palace of Ashes*
Elizabeth Hutner, *Life with Sam*
Joan Cusack Handler, *GlOrious*
Eloise Bruce, *Rattle*
Celia Bland, *Soft Box*
Catherine Doty, *Momentum*
Georgianna Orsini, *Imperfect Lover*
Christopher Matthews, Eye Level, *50 Histories*
Joan Seliger Sidney, *Body of Diminishing Motion*
Christian Barter, *The Singers I Prefer*
Laurie Lamon, *The Fork Without Hunger*
Robert Seder, *To the Marrow*
Andrea Carter Brown, *The Disheveled Bed*
Richard Jeffrey Newman, *The Silence of Men*